Bible Insight

Ross Thompson

Published by Ross Thompson, 2022.

BIBLE INSIGHT

First edition. March 29, 2022.

ISBN: 979-8201900168

Written by Ross Thompson.

Table of Contents

PROOF OF THE DIVINITY OF JESUS

R omans 1:1–4
Paul, a servant of Christ Jesus, called to be an apostle, set apart for the gospel of God, which he promised beforehand through his prophets in the Holy Scriptures, concerning his Son, who was descended from David according to the flesh and was declared to be the Son of God in power according to the Spirit of holiness by His resurrection from the dead, Jesus Christ our Lord,

What do those few verses from Romans one mean? We could paraphrase them by saying; Jesus was proved to be the Son of God when the power of God raised Him from the dead. In His union with the Holy Spirit, death was not able to hold Him because He had never sinned. The New Testament says the sting of death is sin. No sin means no death. Jesus volunteered to die for us.

We can lose sight of the fact the main purpose of the Gospel of Christ is the abolition of death. Paul makes it very clear in his second letter to Timothy.

2 Timothy 1:9,10

The purpose and grace which was given to us in Christ Jesus before time began. But is now made manifest by the appearing of our Saviour Jesus Christ, who hath abolished death, and hath brought life and immortality to light through the gospel.

The Hebrew of the word abolished, means to render inoperative. In the letter to the Hebrews again, Paul explains the purpose of the death, burial and resurrection of Jesus.

Hebrews 2:14,15

Forasmuch then as the children are partakers of flesh and blood, he also himself likewise took part of the same; that through death he might destroy him that had the power of death, that is, the devil; and free those who all their lives were held in slavery by their fear of death.

Let us think back to Christ's crucifixion. What was the immediate major event at Christ's death? It is recorded in Mathew's Gospel.

Mathew 27:50–53

And Jesus cried out again with a loud voice, and yielded up His spirit. Then, behold, the veil of the temple was torn in two from top to bottom; and the earth quaked, and the rocks were split, and the graves were opened; and many bodies of the saints who had fallen asleep were raised; and coming out of the graves after His resurrection, they went into the holy city and appeared to many.

God's immediate response at the very instant of the death of His Son, was the demonstration of the abolition of death. Proof of the successful fulfillment of Christ's mission. The focus then turns to us.

Mathew 10:8

Our job description; *Heal the sick, raise the dead, cleanse the lepers, drive out demons. Freely you have received; freely give.*

That was spoken to the twelve disciples. At the very end of Mathew Jesus instructs the twelve to go to all nations...*teaching them to observe all the commands He had given them.* We are to be ready. alert daily, for these works of power in our relationship with the Father, the Son and the Holy Spirit. Beware of too much knowledge and no power.

1 Corinthians 4:20

For the kingdom of God is not a matter of talk but of power.

THE BEGINNING

The Hebrew name of the book of Genesis is the same as its first word — Bereshit (In the beginning). We can miss the fact water was not created in the seven-day period of the first chapters of Genesis. Genesis one tells us God divided the waters that were already in existence. Both the water and the Earth are included in the first verse. In the beginning God created the heavens and the Earth. That presents a mystery. A firmament was created in Gen 1:6.

The Hebrew הָרָקִיעַ (hā·rā·qî·a') translated 'firmament' is more correctly stated as 'expanse'. That would allow us to conclude the Earth was also in existence from Genesis 1:1. Perhaps God's command for the dry ground to appear (Gen 1:9) was the revealing of the Earth already in existence from Genesis 1:1. I have come to accept the widely held view of a gap between verses one and two of Genesis one.

We are not told when in the beginning is. John's Gospel starts the same way. *In the beginning was the Word, (Jesus) and the Word was with God, and the Word was God. He was in the beginning with God.* Again, we are not told when in the beginning is. It does not refer to God's existence since He is the eternal God. The Hebrew EL used in Genesis is translated God. The Hebrew word Olam in Genesis comes from the root word Im, which means eternity. El Olam in Genesis can be translated eternal, everlasting, forever God. God triune always was and always will be.

The state of the Earth described in verse two seems to indicate an event between the original creation and the Earth being without form and void, covered by the deep, and in darkness. The agreed opinion that God does not create anything chaotic, (without form and void) which the Bible confirms, *For the LORD is God, and he created the heavens and earth and put everything in place. He made the world to be lived in, not to be a place of empty chaos.* Genesis 1:1,2 leads to the conclusion some sort of destructive event caused the first creation to be without form and void. We are seeing the end of a former period and a new beginning.

The Jewish calendar has 2021 as 5781. That is 5781 since the new creation of the first chapters of the Bible. Dinosaur skeletons and bones of other prehistoric animals unearthed in many places around the World seem to have been from a period before this new creation. I think it reasonable to assume the dinosaur age was part of this former period that came to its end in the event that made the Earth without form and void.

Hebrew words for 'without form and void' are: hayah, 'had become' indicating a change from a different state. tohu, 'without form,' confused. Bohu, "void," empty, waste. Choshek, unnatural darkness. Tehowm: an abyss (as a surging mass of water). In the Septuagint (Greek Text) abussos, abyss; the home of demons and evil spirits.

THE FALL

GENESIS THREE describes the events in the garden of Eden at the physical level. We cannot see what is going on in the spiritual realm. Eve, Adam, and the serpent are the dramatis personae. The serpent may have been cunning and crafty, but he was not too bright. He allowed himself to be a party to challenging God. Common sense should have stopped him from bringing calamity upon himself and the others. The serpent can speak. This may indicate all or some of the animals could speak before the disobedience. Eve gives no indication the serpent speaking is other than normal.

God gives us the Bible as an integrated book. We can look to other parts of the Bible to help with the understanding of any section. The rest of the Bible, in many references, tells us the devil used the serpent at this time to induce Eve to disobey God. The serpent consciously allowed the devil to use him, hence his judgment by God. Most of the Bible references to serpents from this point on are synonymous with evil, evil people, or the devil. (2 Corinthians 11:3,4) Paul equates the serpent's temptation of Eve with Church members being enticed away by false teachers. Obviously, Paul is not referring to the animal, rather the devil in false teachers.

(Revelation 12:9,12–15) The devil is called a dragon and a serpent in these verses. Here the devil as all three is the deceiver of the whole world. Eve blames the serpent for deceiving her. (Gen 3:13) Jesus called the Jewish religious leaders a brood of vipers (poisonous snakes). (Mathew 3:7 and 12:34) Jesus equates trampling upon serpents with the power He gives to overcome the devil. (Luke 10:19) Isaiah's description of the new Heaven and Earth (Isa 65:17–25) tells us even then the serpent's food will be dust.

We could paraphrase the serpent's approach to Eve as: "I heard on the grapevine God is not allowing you to eat from any of the trees in the garden. Is that true?". Eve sets him straight regarding the rumor. Only the fruit of the tree of the knowledge of good and evil is forbidden. Her response makes her culpable. It reveals her clear knowledge of what God had forbidden. The serpent calls God a liar and Eve accepts the lie and blatantly disobeys. Adam also rejects God's commandment. (Gen 3:11) and accepts the fruit from Eve and eats.

Eve saw the tree of the knowledge of good and evil as good for food, that it was pleasant to the eyes, and a tree desirable to make one wise. (Gen 3:6) We know the other trees in the garden were good for food. (Gen 1:29) (Gen 2:16) Surely at least some of them must have been pleasant to the eye. What more is needed to make one wise than a relationship with the God who created you? Obviously, Eve did not carefully consider what she already had. The devil was offering her what she already possessed in abundance, His offer was a step down from what she presently enjoyed.

Eating the fruit does not seem to have immediately changed Eve. It is logical to assume if Adam had noticed a change in her he would have been alerted to the dangers of the fruit. I often wonder what the result would have been if Adam had refused the fruit — Eve was disobedient and Adam unchanged? Their eyes were opened after Adam ate. (Gen 3:7)

Unfortunately, they both ate and they both died. The death was a separation from their union with God. They died spiritually and physically. Their bodies which had been eternally alive now began a slow descent into destruction. Spiritually they became united with the devil. God tells Adam he will eventually return to dust. (Gen 3:19) Ephesians 2:1–2 explains the immediate change in Adam and Eve and the entire world. *And you were dead in your trespasses and sins, in which you formerly walked according to the course of this world, according to the prince of the power of the air, of the spirit that is now working in the sons of disobedience.*

This chapter shows Adam and Eve had a massive change in their experience. I have heard it suggested before the fall they were clothed with light. Which has some Scripture support since God Himself dwells in light. (1 Tim 6:16) (Rev 21:23–24) (Rev 22:5) At any rate now they have become excessively self-aware in a way far removed from their previous state. Previously they enjoyed continuous harmony with God. Now they fear Him, knowing something about themselves is opposed to Him.

John G Lake made these comments in one of his sermons: 'The fall of man was his fall into himself. He fell into his own earthly self, out of his heavenly estate, and the separation was absolute and complete. Failure in receiving the Gospel of Jesus in its full truth has one origin — "Man fell into his own earthly self." Our humanity, the I, the self, is the hindrance to accepting all God has for us.

THE WRITING OF MOSES

The events at the conclusion of the Book of Genesis occurred some three hundred years before Moses was born. Obviously, when the heavens and the earth were created nobody witnessed it except God and the heavenly hosts. How then was Moses able to write about the original creation in detail and the rest of the events in Genesis?

There is debate among Scholars that he had some sources, previous writings, to draw upon. I think the most likely explanation is given in 2 Peter 1:21. *For the prophecy came not in old time by the will of man: but holy men of God spoke as they were moved by the Holy Ghost.*

Peter uses the phrase 'in old time' and calls Scripture prophecy. I think we are safe to assume 'old time' refers to all the Old Testament. Moses confirmed that he was a Prophet. *The LORD your God will raise up* for *you a Prophet like me from among you, from your fellow Israelites. You must listen to him.* (Deut. 18:15) This verse itself is a prophecy from Moses. (generally thought to refer to Jesus)

The Jewish calendar has 2021 as 5781. That is from the creation to 2021. Moses lived during the time period between 1550 to 1200 B.C. Jesus authenticated all of Moses' writing as Scripture. *Do not think that I will accuse you to the Father: there is one that accuses you, even Moses, in whom ye trust. For had ye believed Moses, ye would have believed me: for he wrote of me. But if ye believe not his writings, how shall ye believe my words?* (John 5:45–47) *And beginning at Moses and all the prophets, he expounded unto them in all the Scriptures the things concerning himself* (Luke 24:27) The New Testament adds its confirmation to Moses' writing with sixty-three allusions to the first three chapters of Genesis

SEATED PRIEST FINISHED WORK

(John 19:29,30) *So they soaked a sponge in the wine, put it on a stalk of hyssop, and lifted it to His mouth. When Jesus had received the sour wine, He said, "It is finished." And bowing His head, He yielded up His spirit.*

A guest lecturer while I was in Bible College, delivered only two lectures. We discovered later the College President had asked him to demonstrate extreme examples of good homiletics. Seated Priest Finished Work was the title of the first lecture. He must have repeated the phrase twenty times. His text was (Hebrews 10:11,12). *Day after day every priest stands to minister and to offer again and again the same sacrifices, which can never take away sins.* But when this Priest (Hebrews 3: *Jesus is called the High Priest of our profession)had offered for all time one sacrifice for sins, He sat down at the right hand of God....*

The Old Testament Priests could not sit during their continuous daily tasks. And after all that activity, their ministrations were never enough to deal with sin permanently. They are a type of human attempt to accomplish what only God could do. Jesus on the other hand was able to sit down after His Priestly work. Why? Because this Priest had offered for all time one sacrifice for sins.

As a young Student, I did not grasp the full import of the lecturer's oft repeated phrase, "Seated Priest Finished Work." These days I do. Undoubtedly I have more to learn about it, but I do understand now something of the enormity of the finished work of Jesus. This finished work by the Son of God was such that many teachers over the years since His suffering, death, burial, and resurrection, have not been able to cope with it in their human thinking.

The result has been unbiblical teaching encapsulated in such phrases as; Christians are still sinners but forgiven, Christians must confess their sins daily, Christians still have a sin nature. It has also crept into at least one Bible translation. The New Amplified Bible (1 John 2:2) talks about 'the sins of all believers throughout the whole world.' A small thing you might say! It is never a small thing to water down the record of the finished work of the Divine Son of God.

(!John 3:9) states, (Not the New Amplified Bible) *Whoever has been born of God does not sin, for His seed remains in him; and he cannot sin, because he has been born of God.* Such was the accomplishment of Jesus. His atonement was a Divine work, a work of God. We should be careful to come up to it, and careful not to pull it down to our level.

In the original Greek, Hebrews 9:26 says, Jesus appeared ...to do away with sin by the sacrifice of Himself. To do away with sin in all its forms, for those who receive His atonement. Hebrews 9:28 in the Hebrew language says, Jesus appeared once to put away sin and He will come a second time to see the sinless salvation of those who are waiting for Him.

DOES DEATH DELIVER FROM SIN

I read this statement today: (which I do not agree with) **The sin nature is not eradicated from the believer during his time on earth, nor is it ever reformed, as though it can be made to love God** If I was face to face with this speaker I would have a question. If that is so, when does the sin nature leave the believer? The logical answer has to be - at death. Adam Clark, in his Commentary, was of the opinion that idea has more holes in it than a Swiss cheese

FROM THE COMMENTARY: Nothing is purified by death; nothing in the grave; nothing in heaven. Because they think no man can be fully saved from sin in this life. I ask, where is this in unequivocal words, written in the New Testament? Where, in that book is it intimated that sin is not wholly destroyed till death takes place, and the soul and the body are separated? Nowhere!

Sin defaced the divine image; Jesus came to restore it. Sin must have no triumph; and the Redeemer of mankind must have his glory. But if man be not perfectly saved from all sin, sin does triumph, and satan exult, because they have done a mischief that Christ either cannot or will not remove. To say he cannot, would be shocking blasphemy against the infinite power and dignity of the great Creator; to say he will not, would be equally such against the infinite benevolence and holiness of his nature. All sin, whether in power, guilt, or defilement is the work of the devil; and He, Jesus, came to destroy the work of the devil; and as all unrighteousness is sin, so his blood cleanses from all sin, because it cleanses from all unrighteousness.

CONTINUED: Some do hold out death as the complete deliverer from all corruption, and the final destroyer of sin, as if it were revealed in every page of the Bible! Whereas there is not one passage in the sacred volume that says any such thing. Were this true, then death, far from being the last enemy, would be the last and best friend, and the greatest of all deliverers: for if the last remains of all the indwelling sin of all believers is to be destroyed by death, then death, that removes it, must be the highest benefactor of mankind. The truth is, death is neither the cause nor the means of its destruction. It is the blood of Jesus alone that cleanses from all unrighteousness.

LATER IN THE PASSAGE HE ADDS: And what can be said more of the whole herd of transgressors and infidels? They cease to sin when they cease to breathe? Unquote.

Jesus made the whole issue very clear. (John 8:24) *Therefore I said to you that you will die in your sins; for if you do not believe that I am He, you will die in your sins.*" Only one group carry sin in themselves to the next life. Those who do not accept His salvation.

The Apostle Paul: (Romans 8:23*) Not only so, but we ourselves, who have the first fruits of the Spirit, groan inwardly as we wait eagerly for our adoption to sonship, to wit, the redemption of our bodies.* No mention of a believer's sin nature here. Paul continues with his theme through Romans 7 and 8. The sin corrupted body is the last vestige of sin to go. We wait only for the redemption of our bodies.

PERFECTION IN THE BIBLE

Here in Australia a few years ago it was common to see a bumper sticker that read: 'Christians are not perfect just forgiven'. The Bible says the opposite. Way back in the book of Genesis, God said to Abraham: *And after he began to be ninety and nine years old, the Lord appeared to him: (Abraham)and said unto him: I am the Almighty God: walk before me, and be perfect* (Genesis 17:1) Adam Clark tackled the subject in his Commentary.

Quote: Many stagger at the term perfection in Christianity; because they think that what is implied in it is inconsistent with a state of probation, and savors of pride and presumption: but we must take good heed how we stagger at any word of God; and much more how we deny or fritter away the meaning of any of His sayings, lest he reprove us, and we be found liars before him. But it may be that the term is rejected because it is not understood. Let us examine its import.

The word 'perfection,' in reference to any person or thing signifies that such person or thing is complete or finished; that it has nothing redundant, and is in nothing defective. And hence that observation of a learned civilian is at once both correct and illustrative, namely, 'We count those things perfect which want nothing requisite for the end whereto they were instituted.' And to be perfect often signifies 'to be blameless, clear, irreproachable;' and according to the above definition of Hooker, a man may be said to be perfect who answers the end for which God made him.

And as God requires every man to love him with all his heart, soul, mind, and strength, and his neighbour as himself; then he is a perfect man that does so; he answers the end for which God made him; and this is more evident from the nature of that love which fills his heart:

for as love is the principle of obedience, so he that loves his God with all his powers, will obey him with all his powers; and he who loves his neighbour as himself will not only do no injury to him but, on the contrary, labour to promote his best interests.

Why the doctrine which enjoins such a state of perfection like this, should be dreaded, ridiculed, or despised, is a most strange thing; and the opposition to it can only be from that carnal mind that is enmity to God; 'That is not subject to the law of God, neither indeed can be.' Unquote

Hebrews tells us the purpose of Jesus' atonement was to make believers perfect. The Law failed to do that. (Hebrews 10:1) The law is only a shadow of the good things that are coming — not the realities themselves. For this reason it can never, by the same sacrifices repeated endlessly year after year, make perfect those who draw near to worship.

(Hebrews 10:14) *For by one sacrifice he (Jesus)has made perfect forever those who are being made holy.* In God's eyes genuine believers in Christ are perfect the instant they receive Jesus' salvation.

SORTING OUT 1 JOHN CHAPTER ONE.

A doctrine has been made from a few verses in 1 John 1: 7–10; *But if we walk in the light as He is in the light, we have fellowship with one another; and the blood of Jesus Christ His Son cleanses us from all sin. If we say that we have no sin, we deceive ourselves, and the truth is not in us. If we confess our sins, He is faithful and just to forgive us our sins and to cleanse us from all unrighteousness. If we say that we have not sinned, we make Him a liar, and His word is not in us.*

These verses are used to support the teaching that Christians should always be confessing their sins, to receive cleansing and stay in right relationship with God. To put it another way; Christians must be preoccupied with their sins daily in order receive forgiveness and cleansing. The first problem with this teaching is that it does not consider the information in other parts of the 1John letter. A discussion or conclusion is not valid unless all available information on the subject at hand has been considered.

As an example, let's take chapter 1:10; *If we say we have not sinned, we make Him a liar and the truth is not in us,* and chapter 2:1; *These things I write to you that you may not sin. And if anyone sins, we have an advocate with the Father, Jesus Christ the righteous.* John is giving one of his reasons for writing the letter; that his readers may not sin. If they give attention to his writing they will live without sinning. Doesn't that imply a contradiction to what he says in the previous verse? If I am able to live today without sinning because of John's letter, does that mean that I call God a liar if I tell somebody today that I have not sinned? Also, if John is able to write a letter which can result in his readers not sinning, then to have that ability, he himself must be living without sinning. John obviously believed it was possible to live without sinning.

If we compare other parts of the 1 John letter with the teaching that Christians are always sinning and needing to confess, we will find that teaching has very little support. Here is a brief list; 3:6 *Whoever abides in Him does not sin. Whoever sins has neither seen Him or known Him. 3:8 Whoever sins is of the devil. 3:9 Whoever has been born of God does not sin, for His seed remains in him; and he cannot sin, because he has been born of God. 5:18 We know that whoever is born of God does not sin; but he who has been born of God keeps himself, and the wicked one does not touch him.*

How then, do we interpret those first few verses in chapter 1? Talking about Jesus in 1 John 1:2,3 John says, *the life was manifested, and we have seen, and bear witness, and declare to you that eternal that was with the Father and was manifested to us — that which we have seen and heard we declare to you, that you may have fellowship with us; and truly our fellowship is with the Father and with His Son Jesus Christ.* He is talking to those who do not yet have fellowship with the Father and Jesus. In short, he is preaching the Gospel to unsaved people.

1 John 1:1–10 is exhortation from John to accept what God has said in the Gospel. All are sinners needing a savior. If we say we have never sinned we make God a liar, with regard to what he has said in the Gospel. If we admit that we are sinners as the Gospel says, and confess our sins, God is faithful and just to forgive us ours sins and to cleanse us by the blood of Jesus. If we say we don't need the Gospel we deceive ourselves. The Amplified Bible uses the words 'truth of the Gospel' or 'the message of the Gospel', three times in those verses.

One further reference outside of 1 John will help to dispel this teaching of a life of introspection by Christians. Paul gives us a brief description of his personal life with God in 1 Corinthians 4:3; *'But with me it is a very small thing that I should be judged by you or by a human court. In fact, I do not even judge myself. For I know nothing against myself, yet I am not justified by this; but he who judges me is the Lord'.* No introspection or concern about his standing with God there. '*I do not even judge myself'.* It is a description of a life lived in unconcerned trust in God.

This discussion shows us God expects us to read carefully and thoughtfully. We have to use out 'thinker' when reading the Bible. Should we blame those who taught us wrongly here? No! We have our own Bible and God expects us to study it, and confirm for ourselves the truth of what we hear.

TROUBLE WITH EVIL SPIRITS - RESOURCES

A RESOURCE

If you are being harassed by evil spirits, you have come to this article looking for answers. And you want something that works. You will find what you need in the second section of this story (below). For new Christians and others not familiar with the concept of the believers' authority in Christ, I suggest starting with this resource. It will give you a Biblical education on our authority and enable you to get results at the same time. It is a simple website. www.thedeliverancewebsite.com The site contains a free deliverance audio by Apostle Terry Dunn. It is just over one hour in length and covers all bases regarding deliverance. All the listener needs do is listen to Apostle Terry and agree with his prayers and proclamations. It is a simple site with a short video introduction by Apostle Terry before and after the audio. The audio has helped many people

The main thought of the rest of this article can be condensed into one sentence. If you are a Christian, you can bind evil spirits in the name of Jesus and stop them harassing you. It is a basic right we all have as Christians.

That truth is found in Mathew 16:18,19. I am focusing on the 'binding' element of the verses in this article. I encourage you the reader to seek God for revelation and understanding on 'loosing'. I am doing that myself. Throughout the many years since being born again I have experienced disturbance and abuse from evil spirits. The Lord has kept me and enabled me to grow in grace, but it is true to say much of my daily life was adversity and affliction.

I could never understand why Christians around me seemed to be breezing through life relatively trouble free, while I was often embarrassed by attacks and pressures I could hardly cope with. So, if you are in that sort of situation be encouraged you are not alone. Somewhere in the New Testament is a verse that says: *"Knowing that the same sufferings are happening to your brothers and sisters around the world."* One of the devils lies is that we are the only person suffering these things. Admittedly, having that knowledge does not make the trials we are going through easier.

Over time I learned I had authority over evil in Jesus name and did my best to exercise that authority. I read books, received from Ministries and did everything I could think of to win against the enemy. The New Testament is very clear we have authority in Jesus. We are winners in the victory Jesus won. It is extremely important we accept that authority and begin to exercise it through declaration of the word and prayer. We are then having the faith God requires of us, and we have accepted the revelation of His word. I was standing up against the enemy which assured me of Gods help because the two things He expects of us are acceptance of His word and faith.

I was winning but the battles continued, and generally my life was stressful and disrupted. As I became stronger in exercising authority in Jesus, the enemy switched the attacks to night-time, and during my sleep — when I could not consciously defend myself. After many years I was told about John Eckhardt's book 'Prayers to Rout demons.' and began to use it before sleeping. A protective night declaration from the book: "I bind any attack upon my life at night." That decree and some others was immediately effective and took a lot of pressure off me. The book and Apostle Terry Dunns' website (free audio) are very effective resources. The free audio in particular will do a clean sweep of your life, giving you the assurance, everything needing to be dealt with has been attended to. The blessing of the audio is that Apostle Terry does all the work. We have all listened to so many sermons we have an unconscious aversion to long speeches. With this audio it's as if the Lord is saying, "Here, I have made it easy for you. All you need to do is listen and agree."

While using Apostle Eckhardt's book the question occurred to me one day, "Why am I not doing this myself, without the book?" Then I began to think about Mathew 16:18–19. As I meditated on the verses, I began to see the importance of these words of Jesus. I want to briefly take a closer look at the verses.

Firstly, Jesus is talking about the number one item on Gods to do list — building His church *"And on this rock (Himself) I will build My church." Then He declares it will be a winning church (that's us!!) and hell will be unable to stand against it.* "And the gates of hell shall not prevail against it." Prevail means to hold out against or gain mastery. He then brings us into it and explains we will need the keys of the Kingdom of Heaven to be a part of this success against hell. *"And I will give unto you the keys of the Kingdom of Heaven."* Notice Jesus does not say the keys to the Kingdom of Heaven. We don't need the keys to enter the Kingdom of Heaven. We have access. In fact, Ephesians tells us we are seated in heavenly places in Christ Jesus. Jesus is offering us the keys of the Kingdom of Heaven. That can be explained this way; If you are booked into a hotel, you don't need keys to enter the hotel. You can freely go in and out, but you don't have the keys to all the doors in the hotel. The Lord is saying "you are in the Kingdom of Heaven, but you need keys to get the things that are in heaven into your life." He says they are a gift from Him.

Then He tells us what the keys are. *"And whatever you bind on earth will be bound in heaven, and whatever you loose on earth will be loosed in heaven."* Those words can be translated as 'will have been bound in heaven' and 'will have been loosed in heaven.' We can now bring something that has happened in heaven, into our lives on earth by binding and loosing. What has happened in heaven to enable us to bind evil spirits?

(Ephesians 4:8) Therefore He says: *When He (Jesus) ascended on high, He led captivity captive and gave gifts to men."* After Jesus paid the price for our sin, He arose from the dead and when His work on earth was finished, ascended to heaven. He had delivered us from the devil who held us captive because of our sin. Now captivity (the devil) was captive regarding us. Evil has no right to us anymore. That is our status in heaven. We must now bring it into our lives on earth. Jesus established that teaching when He instructed the disciples to pray, *"Our Father who art in heaven hallowed be your name. Your Kingdom come your will be done on earth as it is in heaven."* One of the gifts Jesus gave to men is the power to bind evil spirits. The Lord is saying, "Now your part is to bind and loose."

We do that by speaking in faith. To bind means to tie up as with a rope. Again, the imperative of speaking in faith is taught throughout the New Testament. I will highlight just one. *"But what does it say? The word is near you, in your mouth and in your heart, that is the word of faith which we preach."* (Rom 10:8)

I have succeeded in stopping all spiritual attacks against me using this simple principle. I'm sure I have a lot more to learn about binding. This is how I do it at present. Each morning I say — "In the name of Jesus the Christ, I bind every evil spirit planning to attack my body this day." "In the name of Jesus the Christ, I bind every evil spirit planning to attack my mind this day." "In the name of Jesus the Christ, I bind every evil spirit from being in the atmosphere around me this day."

I do the same thing before going to bed with the addition, "In the name of Jesus the Christ, I bind every evil spirit planning to attack me in my dreams as I sleep." That's it. If you do that in faith it will work for you.

We can also apply this to other parts of our lives where we detect the enemy interfering. I write Christian books and in the past, particularly with the sort of content in this article, I would often get oppressions during the writing. Before starting those books, I bind any and every evil spirit in the name of Jesus from interfering in the writing and publication of the book. Also, from interfering with my computer, with people finding the book online, and with people understanding and applying the teaching. It made a big difference in my experience.

Jesus paid a high price to make these gifts available to us. Let's use them to the full. Evil spirits main tactic against us is fear and bluff. Once you persist in using your authority in Jesus name, your Christian life will change for the better.

JESUS ON MEN LOOKING AT WOMEN

It helps to better understand this statement by Jesus, *"...But I say unto you that whoever looks at a woman to lust for her has already committed adultery with her in his heart."* (Math 5:27,28)

I was at a youth prayer meeting years ago, and somebody asked a Minister who was present for a comment on this verse. My ears pricked up because I was struggling with this issue myself. He replied, "some friends of mine and I discussed this, and we came to agreement that the first look is OK and the second look is lust." Is that really the answer? Is that the best God has for us? I We need to face the fact that we are wired to look and that the ladies are made to cause us to look! How will I know who I am attracted too and who is a potential marriage partner if I don't look? God put sexual attraction in us. It's not going away.

Assuming it was not God's intention to give us the urge so that He could delight in catching us in adultery, or cause us to be tormented all our lives, there must be a better solution.

The key to Jesus' meaning are in the phrases, 'to lust after her' (Amplified says, with evil desire for her) and 'in his heart'.

To paraphrase we could say — he looks at her and would sleep with her if he could because of the evil condition of his heart. Christ is really talking to his listeners about the condition of their hearts. He confirmed it in Mark 7 v 21 *"for from within, out of the heart of men, proceed ....**adulteries**..."* Therefore, looking is not the problem. The condition of the heart is what is important. What then is the satisfactory solution for my experience? Here it is!

The disciples received an experience on the day of Pentecost (Acts 2) that is often overlooked. Peter spoke about it in Acts 15. "...and God gave them (the Gentiles) the Holy Spirit as He did with us.......cleansing (purifying) their hearts by faith." One of the miracles of the New Testament is the pure heart obtained for us by Jesus. Does this make a difference in our looking?

Titus gives us His opinion (1 v 15) "*To the pure in heart and conscience all things are pure.*" Adultery is no longer an issue. I don't struggle to get a pure heart. It is something none of us can do. Peter gave us the key. Purifying their hearts by faith. It was given to the people Peter is talking about. It has been given to us also. Receive it by faith — based on God's Word.

WHAT IS CHRISTIAN LOVE

Love is clearly defined in one chapter of the New Testament. 1Corinthian 13 has it all.

Love endures long and is patient and kind.

Love never is envious nor boils over with jealousy.

Love does not parade itself; it is not puffed up.

Love does not behave rudely.

Love does not seek its own.

Love is not touchy or fretful or resentful.

Love takes no account of the evil done to it — pays no attention to a suffered wrong.

Love does not rejoice in iniquity, but rejoices in the truth.

Love bears all things.

Love believes all things.

Love hopes all things.

Love endures all things.

Love never fails.

The Good News is this love has been put in our hearts by the Holy Spirit who has been given unto us. (Romans 5:5) How do we activate it? By recognizing the real Christian life comes from our Spirit. Natural humanity knows nothing of love. It is practiced like everything else in our Christian life; by faith in God's Word. We are in possession of the above love list. We only have to live it out. Feelings and the human personality are completely inadequate. *But we have the mind of Christ and do hold the thoughts intents and purposes of His heart.* (1Corinthians 2:16 — Amplified Bible)

T L OSBORNS POSITIVE GOSPEL

T.L Osborn and his wife Daisy (both in Heaven now) probably preached, in their lifetime, to more people around the world than any other Ministers. The large number of books and Gospel films they distributed adds to that number. T L describes their basic philosophy; "Daisy and I tell people God values them, that He is not mad at them, and that the price He has paid for them is the proof of their worth."

In his book 'You Are God's Best' he states; "This book is based upon the Good News of the Bible. The news here is all Good. God's plan for you is all Good. He is not mad at you. He loves you like you are and has already paid for every wrong you ever committed. That is what He wants you to know, and He believes in you so much that He thinks you will respond positively to Him, as soon as someone tells you about His love plan."

(continued) " I regret it when I read books or hear speakers spreading suspicion. guilt and fear. I do not believe any good is accomplished by criticism, finding fault, or belittling any human person. The most unregenerate person deserves respect as a creation of God. Every human being deserves my highest respect and most sincere esteem, as one for whom Jesus Christ laid down His life in love." unquote

Because of less than perfect family or life experiences, many Christians come to God with unconscious negative ideas about God as Father. I was one of those, and when I discovered T L Osborn's books I grabbed them with both hands. 'You are God's Best' in particular, I keep on my bookshelf and pull it down when I need reminding God is for me not against me, and He proved it when He sent Jesus for me.

T L wrote about the one time he got in trouble with God. He was starting his big crusades in Thailand, a place known at the time as a hard place to preach the Gospel. Knowing that T L decided he would teach the people first by explaining the Gospel. On his first day, he was shocked to have the people laughing at him and completely rejecting the message. Usually, the power of the Holy Spirit passed through the crowds, healing the sick and getting many saved. He closed the meeting as soon as he could and went straight back to his accommodation to get on his knees before God.

The reply God gave him when he asked what the problem was; "I told you to preach the Gospel. You explained the Gospel." He saw his mistake and went back to preaching. Big results followed. Apparently, at that time anyway, (1960) the Taiwanese people were reluctant for others to see them getting emotional. Once T L went back to preaching his Taiwanese interpreter ran off the stage because he could not stop tears from running down his face. T L Osborn had to stop preaching and go in search of him. He found him hiding under the big outdoor platform.

He finally managed to persuade him to return to the interpreting. That particular incident taught me something. God expects us to put some feeling into our preaching. The Gospel is the most exciting message in the World. Dry dissertations do not do it justice. Daisy Osborn wrote books mainly for women. Her burden was to lift women who came from cultures where they were undervalued. T L himself wrote a book entitled, 'If I Were a Woman'.

Between them, T L and Daisy Osborn wrote around 28 books — great Bible study resources for establishing a mindset of God's positive intentions for us personally and learning faith for the life we are able to live in Him. Most of them are still available from Osborn Ministries, online retailers, and online libraries. Online video sites have many original videos of the Osborn Crusades around the World. LaDonna

Osborn, their daughter, continues to bring Osborn Crusades to needy people around the World.

THE BIBLE ON JESUS RETURN

The Bible teaches a two-fold return of Jesus and a two-fold purpose. Acts chapter one lays the groundwork for the teaching of His second coming. After His resurrection, Jesus appeared to the disciples over a period of forty days and spoke about the kingdom of God and the outpouring of the Holy Spirit.

(Acts1:9–11) *"After saying this, he was taken up into a cloud while they were watching, and they could no longer see him. They were looking intently up into the sky as he was going when suddenly two men dressed in white stood beside them. "Men of Galilee," they said, "why are you standing here staring into heaven? Jesus has been taken from you into heaven, but someday he will return from heaven in the same way you saw him go."*

According to Acts 1:12, this happened on the Mount of Olives. Before His crucifixion, Jesus taught the twelve of the two phases of His second coming.

(John 14:1–3). *I go to prepare a place for you. And if I go and prepare a place for you, I will come again, and receive you unto myself; that where I am, there you may be also."*

Here we are told Christ will appear to gather His church to Himself. Paul described it this way in 1 Thessalonians 4:16–18, *"For the Lord Himself shall descend from Heaven with a shout, with the voice of the archangel, and with the trump of God: and the dead in Christ shall rise first: then we which are alive and remain shall be caught up together with them in the clouds, to meet the Lord in the air: and so shall we ever be with the Lord. Wherefore comfort one another with these words."*

And again in 1 Corinthians 15: 51–53, *"Behold, I show you a mystery; We shall not all sleep, but we shall all be changed, in a moment, in the twinkling of an eye, at the last trump: for the trumpet shall sound, and the dead shall be raised incorruptible, and we shall be changed. For this corruptible must put on incorruption, and this mortal must put on immortality"*

Paul seems to be referring to this first part of the appearance, the catching up of the Church, in Titus 2:13, *"Looking for that blessed hope, and the glorious appearing of the great God and our Saviour Jesus Christ"*

The Greek word used is harpazo, which means 'carry off' or 'snatch up'. Jesus also described another facet of His return which is very different from John 14:1–3.

"For then shall be great tribulation, such as was not since the beginning of the world to this time, no, nor ever shall be. And except those days should be shortened, there should no flesh be saved: but for the elect's sake those days shall be shortened. Then if any man shall say unto you, lo, here is Christ, or there; believe it not. For there shall arise false Christs, and false prophets, and shall show great signs and wonders; insomuch that, if it were possible, they shall deceive the very elect. Behold, I have told you before. Wherefore if they shall say unto you, Behold, he is in the desert; go not forth: behold, he is in the secret chambers; believe it not. For as the lightning comes out of the east, and shines even to the west; so shall also the coming of the Son of man be." (Matthew 24:21–27).

Matthew 25 :31 *"When the Son of man shall come in his glory, and all the holy angels with him, then shall He sit upon the throne of His glory"...... And then shall appear the sign of the Son of man in heaven: and then shall all the tribes of the earth mourn, and they shall see the Son of man coming in the clouds of heaven with power and great glory ...... Behold, He comes with clouds; and every eye shall see Him, and they also which pierced Him: and all kindreds of the earth shall wail because of Him ... "*

In this part of Jesus's return every eye shall see Him. All the tribes of the earth will see Him. All the holy angels accompanying Him seem to mean all the angels of Heaven. Hebrews 12:22 calls them "an innumerable company of angels." The letter to Jude authenticates Enoch's prophecy of ten thousands of the Saints returning with the Lord at this time. At the rapture, the Church will be caught up to meet the Lord in the air. In this second part of the return, the Church will be returning to earth with Jesus. The purpose of the second phase of Jesus' coming is to establish His rule on Earth.

At this time a judgment will take place. The Lord Jesus will sit on the throne of His glory and judge the people of the earth. The metaphor of goats and sheep is used to distinguish the ungodly from the righteous. Those found unworthy will be turned into hell. The righteous to eternal life.

Daniel was told "*Seventy weeks are determined upon thy people and upon thy holy city, to finish the transgression, and to make an end of sins, and to make reconciliation for iniquity, and to bring in everlasting righteousness. To seal up vision and prophecy. And to anoint the Most Holy.*" (Daniel 9: 25)

The idea Christians will be forever in Heaven with God after the rapture is challenged by a passage from Revelation 5:9,10. "*And they sang a new song, saying: "You are worthy to take the scroll and to open its seals because you were slain, and with your blood, you purchased for God persons from every tribe and language and people and nation. You have made them to be a kingdom and priests to serve our God, and they will reign on the earth.*"

A thorough reading of Revelation leads to the inevitable conclusion our final destination is Earth. The Church will be in Heaven for the period of the great tribulation. The Church will return with the Lord for the final judgment. Man was made for the earth. The Saints will return to reign on Earth.

Revelation describes Heaven and Earth as being in close proximity at the time of the new Heaven and the new Earth.

(Revelation 21) "*Then I saw a new heaven and a new earth, for the old heaven and the old earth had disappeared. And the sea was also gone.*

And I saw the Holy City, the New Jerusalem, coming down from God out of heaven like a bride beautifully dressed for her husband......having the glory of God. Her light was like a precious stone, like a jasper stone, clear as crystal."

"I heard a loud shout from the throne, saying, "Look, God's home is now among his people! He will live with them, and they will be his people. God himself will be with them. He will wipe every tear from their eyes, and there will be no more death or sorrow or crying or pain. All these things are gone forever."

"And the one sitting on the throne said, "Look, I am making everything new!" And then he said to me, "Write this down, for what I tell you is trustworthy and true." And he also said, "It is finished! I am the Alpha and the Omega — the Beginning and the End. To all who are thirsty, I will give freely from the springs of the water of life. All who are victorious will inherit all these blessings, and I will be their God, and they will be my children."

ONCE SAVED ALWAYS SAVED ?

Jesus speaking in Revelation 3:5 ; *Yet you have a few people in Sardis who have not soiled their clothes. They will walk with me, dressed in white, for they are worthy. The one who is victorious will, like them, be dressed in white. He who overcomes shall be clothed in white garments, and I will not blot out his name from the Book of Life; but I will confess his name before My Father and before His angels.*

That one verse provides all of the answers to the question. Certain persons who had received Christ's salvation, and had their names written in the book of life in Heaven, were now in danger of having their names blotted erased) out. Once saved always saved is not a teaching found in the Bible. Whoever started that idea was really saying : "how much ignoring of God, and sinning, can I get away with before losing my salvation"?

Christianity is very much a personal relationship with God through Christ. Notice in this verse Jesus knows the people in the Church by name. He uses the phrase 'the one' That is true Christianity. A one on one relationship by each person with God. Apostle John talks about the result God is looking for from the preaching of the Gospel. (1John 1:3) *We proclaim to you what we have seen and heard, so that you also may have fellowship with us. And our fellowship is with the Father and with his Son, Jesus Christ.* John is describing true Christianity.

Psalm 91 has two verses that add more explanation. (Psalm 91:1) *He that dwells in the secret place of the most High shall abide under the shadow of the Almighty. I will say of the LORD, He is my refuge and my fortress: my God; in Him will I trust.* The whole Psalm is written to individuals. It is a personal word from God to each person on Earth. (Psalm 91:14) *Because he has set his love upon me (God), therefore will I deliver him.* The Christian life is the constant continuing choice to love God. To put God first above all things.

It is interesting to note Psalm 91 is God's offered protection from disease, plagues, and pandemics. Personal relationship by act of the will, is the prerequisite for protection.

Some Christians in Sardis had failed to set their love upon God. They were loving the world, sin - whatever. Their inner life with God was gone, to such an extent Jesus called them dead. They were not appreciating the price Jesus paid, the love He showed, to save them.

Paul teaches the principle in the New Testament; *And you, who once were alienated and enemies in your mind by wicked works, Yet now he has reconciled you to himself through the death of Christ in his physical body. As a result, he has brought you into his own presence, and you are holy and blameless as you stand before him without a single fault. if indeed you continue in the faith, grounded and steadfast, and are not moved away from the hope of the gospel which you heard, which was preached to every creature under heaven, of which I, Paul, became a minister.* (Colossians 1: 21–23)

Two ifs. If you continue in the faith. If you are not moved away from the hope of the Gospel. There is wisdom in Paul's letter to the Philippian Christians.

(Amplified Bible) So then, my dear ones, just as you have always obeyed [my instructions with enthusiasm], not only in my presence, but now much more in my absence, continue to work out your salvation [that is, cultivate it, bring it to full effect, actively pursue spiritual maturity] with awe-inspired fear and trembling [using serious caution and critical self-evaluation to avoid anything that might offend God or discredit the name of Christ].

DIVINE SCHOOL OF HARD KNOCKS

A while ago I read the book 'Fragile and Anti Fragile' by Nassim Nicholas Taleb. It turned my mind to thinking about fragile and anti-fragile in relation to Christianity, or more to the point, Christians. You have probably noticed in the New Testament the first Christians were a pretty hardy bunch. They did not run from suffering and hardship. In fact, they welcomed it. Take this passage from Acts 5:41.

At this, they (the Jewish Sanhedrin) yielded to Gamaliel. They called the apostles in and had them flogged. Then they ordered them not to speak in the name of Jesus and released them. The apostles left the Sanhedrin, rejoicing that they had been counted worthy of suffering disgrace for the Name. Every day, in the temple courts and from house to house, they did not stop teaching and proclaiming the good news that Jesus is the Christ.

Flogging was no small matter. We can see it did not deter the twelve at all. The Lord Jesus passed a message to Paul through Ananias recorded in Acts 9: *But the Lord said to Ananias, "Go! This man is my chosen instrument to carry my name before the Gentiles and their kings and before the people of Israel. I will show him how much he must suffer for my name.* It was Paul who wrote in Romans 8:17 17 *Now if we are children, we are heirs — heirs of God and co-heirs with Christ, if indeed we share in his sufferings in order that we may also share in his glory.* He repeated the thought to Timothy (2Tim2:12) *If we endure hardship, we will reign with him. If we deny him, he will deny us.* Have you noticed we do not hear a lot about those verses these days?

Admittedly life was hard for everybody in New Testament times. Law and order as we know it today did not exist. The strongest in terms of fighting men and armaments ruled. To survive you made an alliance with the most powerful and hoped for the best. The writings of the historian Josephus paint an alarming picture of the hazards of life in New Testament times. For the people of those times, including the Christians, hardship was all they knew.

Our mindset on the other hand is affected by the benefits of civilization we enjoy. Law and Order, Medical treatment, financial pensions and benefits, and the like. We are all looking for the easiest and most comfortable life. Hardship and suffering have no place in our thinking. And to a degree that is how it should be. Hardship and suffering if they arrive, hit us hard. For this reason, we do well to take on board some of the New Testament's teachings on the subject. I am not treating this subject lightly. I have had the experience of the previous few sentences many times in my Christian life. I did find there is an infinite difference in going through suffering with God than without Him.

I HAVE two cups in my kitchen. They both look much the same — white — same size — same weight. A hidden difference exists between them. I bought a few of one of them because they were cheap. Not many of those are left. Every time I bang them on a tap accidentally a piece breaks off and I must throw it away. The other cost me ten dollars and it is as tough as old boots. I have accidentally knocked it many times and thought uh oh! There goes my ten dollars. But to my surprise, it has survived without even the slightest chip.

What am I getting at here? The Bible calls us vessels (cups) for the Masters (God) use. As we look at the New Testament we can see that the first Christians; Paul, Peter, the other Disciples, and the early Church were far from fragile vessels for God. They took a lot of knocks and it did not break them — in fact, they expected tough times. It is easy to skip over some of the things the New Testament tells us they went through.

James chapter 1:2–4 gives us an idea of their mindset. *Brothers, is your life full of difficulties and temptations? Then be happy, for when the way is rough, your patience has a chance to grow. So, let it grow, and don't try and squirm out of your problems. For when your patience is finally in full bloom, then you will be ready for anything, (not fragile) strong in character, full and complete'. Others echo his comments, 1 Peter chapter 1: 6–7; So be truly glad! There is wonderful joy ahead, even though the going is rough for a while down here. These trials are only to test your faith to see if it is strong and pure. It is being tested as fire tests gold and purifies it.......*

We don't always understand and appreciate that God is constantly working in our lives to turn us from fragile vessels to anti-fragile vessels for Him. From vessels that are easily broken to vessels that are as tough as old boots for God

We must believe God is in control of the smallest aspects of our lives. If He sees fit to lead us into the School of Hard Knocks, we should not be surprised. Peter's further advice to the Christians in his first letter; *Beloved, don't be surprised at the fiery trial which is to try you, as though some strange thing happened unto you.*

YOUR DIRECT PERSONAL SERVICE TO GOD

The Bible has passages that point the way to direct personal service to God. For example; (Psalm 19:17) *He that has pity on the poor lends to the LORD; and that which he has given will he pay him again.*

(Mathew 25:32–40) Has six more ways to serve God personally and directly. *All the nations will be gathered before Him (the King), and He will separate the people one from another, as a shepherd separates the sheep from the goats. He will place the sheep on His right and the goats on His left.*

Then the King will say to those on His right, "Come, you who are blessed by My Father, inherit the kingdom prepared for you from the foundation of the World. For I was hungry and you gave Me something to eat, I was thirsty and you gave Me something to drink, I was a stranger and you took Me in, I was naked and you clothed Me, I was sick and you looked after Me, I was in prison and you visited Me."

Then the righteous will answer Him, "Lord, when did we see You hungry and feed You, or thirsty and give You something to drink? When did we see You a stranger and take You in, or naked and clothe You? When did we see You sick or in prison and visit You?

And the King will reply, 'Truly I tell you, whatever you did for one of the least of these brothers of Mine, you did for Me."

Feed the hungry, give drink to the thirsty, Taking strangers in, clothing the naked, ministering to the sick, visiting prisoners. Are these verses talking about Christians helping Christians? Personally I think Yes, but it also includes helping needy people where ever we find them. The New Testament exhortations not to neglect to show hospitality to strangers, and to heal the sick are for all people. The large majority of the people Jesus healed were not believers. He met peoples needs where-ever He found them, as a witness to the Kingdom of God and the truth of Himself as the Messiah.

When-ever the Bible mentions the poor, it makes no distinction between the believing poor and the unbelieving poor. I think we are safe to follow these seven paths where- ever we find them. And what a blessing. To be able to minister directly to the Lord Himself.

THE GREAT LOVE WORK OF GOD

(2 Corinthians 5:14) For Christ's love compels us, because we are convinced that One died for all, therefore all have died. And He died for all, that those who live should no longer live for themselves, but for Him who died for them and was raised again...

This verse has always fascinated me. It is stunning, the enormity of the truth it conveys. The best way to see it clearly, I think, is to paraphrase it piece by piece. So to start; Paul says Christ's love compels us because... Something God has done in His love for the World compels us to preach the Gospel. What is that something?

Paul says we are convinced or persuaded about a true fact; that one died for all. We are convinced that it is true. Jesus died for all. For every man, woman, boy, and girl, who has ever lived, is living at present, and who will yet be born. What an enormous work of God. One died for the total number of people who have been born on this earth. Paul is saying the enormity and scope of this work of the love of God, is what pushes us out to tell people about it, and to persuade them to take hold of it for themselves.

The Apostle then moves to a fact that has always astounded me. If one has died for all, the logical conclusion is that all have died (in Christ). Have you ever thought about this statement? The next time you go to the shops, or to work, or any place where people are, look around at the people and think to yourself — 'they have all already died in Christ.' They have all died, says Paul. That is how close people are to salvation. All they need do is genuinely say, "Yes God, I'll take Jesus' salvation." In that instant, their death in Christ is applied to their lives.

Paul then strikes a blow to the Universalist's doctrine. They say because Jesus died for all, everybody is saved or eventually will be saved.

The Scottish clergyman George MacDonald, whom C S Lewis has as a character in his book 'The Great Divorce,' held the Universalist doctrine. Mac Donald wrote many books including works of fantasy, which especially impressed Lewis. He does say clearly in his writing that MacDonald was a Universalist.

When Paul says, 'that those who live' he is separating out a group of persons from the 'all' Christ died for. He means those who have taken Jesus' salvation and therefore have obtained eternal life. All have died in Christ but sadly not all have received it in a genuine act of their will. In the next few verses beyond this passage, Paul makes an impassioned plea to everybody, *'be reconciled to God'*.

The Apostle concludes with something which was glaringly obvious in his life, and which he takes to be the bottom line for all of us. Because of this great love work of God, we should no longer live for ourselves, which is what non-Christian people do. But hand our lives over to Him who died and was raised for us, and to present ourselves as clay, available to be molded in the Divine Potters hands.

THE EXCHANGED LIFE

A mentor of mine once told me of a conversation he had with a fellow Minister. The two of them were travelling, speaking in churches, and staying in the homes of a member of each Church. One morning they had just got on the road and my friend sensed tension between them. The other Minister seemed to be unhappy with my friend. He asked if there was something wrong, had he done something to offend his companion? The answer was that his travelling companion had noticed he had not had a morning quiet time. He was quite upset about it, presumably because he believed they were not right with God and their ministry at the Churches would suffer. I can't recall my mentor's exact answer, but I have a fair idea of what he would have said.

There is certainly nothing wrong with having a morning quiet time or a time set apart to God each day. The Ministers mistake was in his thinking. He had made it a rule or a law. ' I am not right with God if I don't have a morning quiet time every day.' God will be unhappy with me and my Christian life will suffer. A similar idea — if I don't spend some separate time with God daily I am starting to fall away from Him. The truth is even if I do have a quiet time or separate time alone with God daily, it doesn't come close to God's expectations of us in our relationship with Him. The implication behind these rules about time with God is that God and I are separate. He is in Heaven and I am down here, and it is my responsibility to make sure I make contact at least once a day. I can then carry on with my life secure that I have done what is required of me.

You would struggle to find backing for that idea in the New Testament. It is more of an Old Testament concept. God was external to them and they were tasked by Him to practise external activities to keep themselves in His favour. The Old Testament is full of all the external practises required of them. Although Jesus taught often of His inner relationship with His father; *"The Father who is in me He does the works" (John 5:19) "Do you not believe that I am in the Father and the Father in me?"* (John 14:10) For the disciples, it was still an external relationship for most of their time with Jesus. It was only as the time for His crucifixion drew near that He began to teach them of an internal relationship for them. "The Spirit of truth whom the world cannot receive, because it neither sees Him or knows Him: but you know Him, for He dwells with you and will be in you." (John 14:17) He prayed to the Father that they might have that inner relationship. *"That they all may be one, as you, Father, are in Me, and I in you; that they also may be one in Us, that the world may believe that you sent me."* (John 17:21)

The change from the Old Testament relationship and the New came soon after Jesus' resurrection from the dead. *"When He had said this, He showed them His hands and His side. Then the disciples were glad when they saw the Lord. So, Jesus said to them again, peace to you! As the Father has sent Me, even so send I you. And when He had said this, He breathed on them, and said to them receive the Holy Spirit. If you forgive the sins of any they are forgiven them; if you retain the sins of any, they are retained."* (John 20:21–23) Suddenly they are thrust into a new inner relationship with the Father, and a responsibility to do the works of God through that relationship. God's prophecy to Jeremiah is fulfilled. *"But this is the covenant I will make with the house of Israel after those days, says the Lord; I will put My law in their minds, and write it on their hearts; and I will be their God, and they shall be My people."* (Jer 31:33)

More than an inner relationship, and this is my point, the disciples received a transferred life. They had become a new creation. They were now Christ people — twenty-four hours a day, seven days a week. Paul explained this life as the basic result of the Gospel. *"For the love of Christ compels us, because we thus judge: that if one died for all, then have all died; and He died for all, so that all those who live may not live unto themselves, but unto Him who died and rose again for their sake."* (2Cor 5:14,15) *He explained his life this way, "I have been crucified with Christ: it is no longer I who live, but Christ lives in me: and the life which I now live in the flesh I live by the faith of the Son of God, who loved me and gave Himself for me."* (Gal 2:20)

Certainly, it is a life to be learned. Johns Gospel in the first chapter says, *"But as many as received Him, (Jesus) to them He gave the right to become the children of God, to those who believe in His name."* (:12) When we first come to Jesus we are aware only of ourselves and our body. We then need to learn to become Sons of God, to learn to live in the Spirit in daily discipleship to our indwelling God. Romans 8:4 tells us *"The righteous requirement of the law has been fulfilled in us who do not walk according to the flesh but according to the Spirit."* We have no more laws to keep, only a relationship to be lived out. The new believer must learn to live moment by moment with God within.

The goal is to enter the relationship Jesus modeled for us with His Father. *"Phillip said to Him, Lord show us the Father and it will be sufficient for us. Jesus said to him, have I been with you so long and yet you have not known me, Phillip? He who has seen me has seen the Father; so how can you say, show us the Father. Do you not believe that I am in the Father, and the Father in me? The words that I speak to you I do not speak on my own authority; but the Father who dwells in me does the works."* (John 14:8–10)

The believer's whole life becomes a quiet time with God. Paul called it the communion of the Holy Spirit. (2 Cor 13:14) *"For as many as are led by the Holy Spirit, these are the Sons of God."* (Rom 8:14) It is largely a hidden life very often not seen or appreciated by others. If Jesus' inner life with His Father was not understood by those around Him, we should not expect our lives to be any different. The Minister who was upset with my friend because of his failure to have a quiet time was well off the mark. My mentor was a spiritual man committed to a disciple relationship with God. Perhaps the Holy Spirit had instructed him to lie awake most of the night and pray. Maybe God had kept him awake and given him the message he was to speak at the next Church. The Lord might have said to him, "I want you to praise me in the Spirit for a few hours tonight." Which made him tired, or late getting up in the morning.

My point is that his was a continuing relational experience with God. His only law was the *"Law of the Spirit of life in Christ Jesus."* (Rom 8:2) Jesus came to restore to us a Spiritual life lived in relationship with Himself, the Father, and the Holy Spirit. Every minute of every day.

WITH SHOUTS OF GRACE GRACE

The title comes from Zechariah 4:7 in the Old Testament.

"For I am the least of the apostles, who am not fit to be called an apostle, because I persecuted the church of God. But by the grace of God I am what I am, and His grace toward me did not prove vain; but I labored even more than all of them, yet not I, but the grace of God that is with me". (1Cor 15:9,10) His deliverance from an ungodly life, his work and his identity, Paul explains, are the result of God's grace. Gods undeserved favor (grace) saved him. His ability to serve God is the grace of God that is within him. His selfhood — his personality, is a product of the grace of God. *"By the grace of God, I am what I am".*

Paul's life presented to us in the New Testament, is an example, a template if you like, of the Christian life that is pleasing to God. We don't know if it took some time for Paul to understand the grace life or whether he had a revelation from the Lord about it. We do have examples of prominent Christians nearer to our time who had to learn the lesson of the exchanged life lived by grace.

Saved as a child, an Englishman, Major Ian Thomas, in 1933 at age 19 became a windmill of activity, his life packed tight with feverish activity: preaching, talking, counselling with passionate desire to win souls for Christ. But he found the more he did, the more energy he expended, the less happened.

He states: "I became deeply depressed, because I loved the Lord Jesus Christ with all my heart; I wanted to be made a blessing to my fellow men. But I discovered that forever doubling and redoubling my efforts to win souls, rushing here and dashing there, taking part in this campaign, taking part in that campaign, preaching in the morning, preaching in the evening, talking to the Bible class, witnessing to this one, counselling with another, did nothing, nothing — nothing to change the utter barrenness, the emptiness, the uselessness of my activity. I tried to make up with noise what I lacked in effectiveness and power".

Worn out after seven years he was ready to give up. Then the Lord Jesus spoke to him "You have been busy trying to do for Me all that only I can do through you. Now supposing I am your life, and you begin to accept it as a fact, then I am your strength! You have been pleading and begging for that for seven years. I am your victory in all areas of your life, if you want it! I am the One to whom it is perfectly natural to go out and win souls; and I know precisely where to go and find them. Why don't you begin to reckon upon Me and say thank you"?

Another of the Lord's statements to him caught my attention. "Now you have to realize; you cannot have My life for your program. You can only have My life for My program". Major Ian Thomas went to be with the Lord at the age of 92yrs after a full life of writing, and Ministry around the world. *

As always Jesus is our foremost example of a life submitted to God's grace. He chose to be fully available to His Father. Christ's life on earth was a commitment to the Father's program. "Jesus therefore answered and was saying to them, *Truly, truly, I say to you the Son can do nothing of Himself, unless it is something He sees the Father doing; for whatever the Father does, these things the Son also does in like manner*". (John 5:19) It is remarkable that He submitted His speech to His Father also. *"For I did not speak on my own initiative, but the Father himself who sent Me has given Me commandment, what to say, and what to speak"*. (John 12:49)

Many preachers throughout history have discovered that to be effective they needed to wait on God, listen, and speak only that which God had given them, F. F. Bosworth, an Evangelist in the U.S. in the early 1900s, had many healings accompany his preaching. Each night when conducting outreaches, he placed a pad and pen near his bed.

God woke him in the night and gave him the next day's sermon. He wrote it all down and went back to sleep. That sermon preached the next day always produced mighty results for the Kingdom of God.

It would be a mistake to think that submission to the grace of God is a passive humdrum existence. Paul explained in the reference at the beginning of this article, making himself available to God's grace enabled him to work harder than all the other apostles. John tells us if all the works of Jesus were recorded the world would not be enough to accommodate all the books. (John 21:25) Jesus obviously saw the Father in constant activity.

Have you noticed the weakest and most unlikely people are God's choice for his biggest works? After teaching them to be available to his grace within them, an explosion of his activity through them is the result. T.L.Osborn the seventh son of a struggling farming family, had travelled no further than the nearest town before God called him. Oral Roberts was a stuttering student dying of tuberculosis. Kenneth Hagin, a young man bedridden with a serious heart condition. Benny Hinn also stuttered and lacked confidence. An impoverished, timid, farmer's wife, Maria Woodworth Etter struggled to obey God's call to preach when very few women were in positions of prominence. Kenneth and Gloria Copeland continually battled financial failure. God used all these and many more like them, once His grace had free rein in them, to save, heal, and bless millions.

Apostle Neil Thomas, a mentor of mine, whom God used to plant churches in the South Pacific, would often say," I just walk around behind the Holy Spirit. A few times he said to me after a great teaching session, "You could do this Ross — it's by God's grace". I have heard David Herzog say, "God does it all and makes me look good." The truth is we are all in the same boat with those chosen by God for huge ministries. 2 Corinthians 4:7 says, *"For we have this treasure (God's presence) in earthen vessels (us) that the surpassing greatness of the power might be of God and not from ourselves"*.

Whether called to minister to millions, or like most of us, our service for God is to workmates and neighbours; we will not have the satisfaction of seeing lasting results if we don't embrace the truth of the operation of God's grace working in us. "It is the Spirit who gives life; the flesh profits nothing; the words that I have spoken unto you are spirit and they are life". (John 6:63) If we wish to offer life to the spiritually dead around us it must happen through our availability to, and union with the Holy Spirit. It is a life that is learned as we make ourselves available to a close relationship with the Father, Son and Holy Spirit.

If you study the lives of those used by God in large ministries their availability and dependence upon God quickly becomes obvious. I was watching a video of Kenneth Copeland preaching in Africa. He stopped in mid sermon and asked the Lord how to continue in his next comments. He waited in silence listening. After a moment he said, "Thank you sir", and continued with the sermon.

A lady with an evil spirit had come on stage at a Benny Hinn open-air meeting I attended in Australia. He described the Holy Spirit's instruction to him about the evil spirit, and before casting it out said the Holy Spirit was telling him to stand back. That surprised me. I realized then how available, dependent, and obedient these Ministers need to be.

Wanting to be sure his ministry will have God's power, Brazilian evangelist Carlos Anacondia often hangs back on decisions about the work until God presses him about it. That way he is sure he is in the flow of God's grace and sure of results. Again, when I read that it surprised me because my thinking was that I should get moving as soon as I had the slightest clue what God wanted me to do. Annacondia knows only God's program wins souls, and he takes care to be in alignment with it.

Paul worked harder than the other apostles by God's grace, but he also knew how to sit still when God asked it of him. Acts 19:9,10 tells us Paul stopped his evangelistic travelling at one point and spent two years in the one place teaching the word and praying for the people. His agenda was God's agenda, not his own. In two verses Ephesians 2:8,9 sums up the whole principle of living in God's grace. *"For by grace you are saved through faith, and that not of yourselves; it is the gift of God, not of works, lest anyone should boast.*

THE VOICE WITHIN

Something John G Lake said in one of his sermons, gave me a new perspective on what is important in my Christian life. "I tell you, beloved, the external evidence's of God and the power of His Spirit, no matter how wonderful, are a small matter compared with the consciousness of the Word of God in the human heart, in your heart and mine, bless God."

Jesus said, My sheep listen to My voice; I know them, and they follow Me. I give them eternal life, and they will never perish. No one can snatch them out of My hand. (John 10:27) Some have heard God speak to them in an audible voice. A friend of mine was laying on his couch one day, and God told him in an audible voice to get up, go to the City, and preach the Gospel to a certain group of people.

It seems God's audible voice is in the main, a rare event. How do most of us hear God's voice then? Within ourselves, in our spirits. The Bible says God is a Spirit. The Spirit realm is the main realm from God's point of view. Heaven is a Spiritual place. In the above verse, Jesus made the distinction between the Godly and the Un-Godly. Those who have God in their lives and those who do not. The Bible describes the Un-Godly as being In the World without God and without hope. (Ephesians 2:12)

In other words, millions of people Worldwide live without God, hoping everything will be OK. Hoping the throw of the dice will come up good for them. Godly hope is an experience of surety, springing from a relationship with God through Jesus. Inability to hear God's voice can have deadly consequences. George G Ritchie, the author of the book 'Return from Tomorrow' tells of an experience as a soldier, near the front lines in World War 2. Exhausted from days of frontline engagement, he and his fellow soldiers were happy to board a truck designated to transport them away from the front lines, for a few days of rest and recreation.

George was one of the last aboard. Just getting comfortable, he heard God say within him, "Get off the truck." George was most unhappy about that and resisted for a while. Finally, he responded to the prompt and glumly watched another soldier take his place. The truck moved off. An hour or so later a message came through saying the truck had run over a landmine and all aboard had been killed. 'Return from Tomorrow' tells how George Ritchie caught pneumonia and died, at a WW2 army training camp. He left his body, had an encounter with Jesus, and finally found his way back to his body, where the medics had decided to try one more shot of adrenalin, which got his heart pumping again.

It is a faith-building book and ideal to give to non-Christians. The Apostle John spoke of what is of first importance for any human being, and the main reason for the proclamation of the Gospel. We proclaim to you what we have seen and heard, so that you also may have fellowship with us. And this fellowship of ours is with the Father and with His Son, Jesus Christ. (1John 1:3) I had been a Christian a few years before I noticed John was not speaking of Christians fellowshipping together. Our fellowship is with God the Father and with His Son, Jesus Christ. Fellowship with God (companionship, friendship, walking together) is the first priority of the Gospel. That obviously implies communication, speech, and conversation.

I agree with John G Lake. It is a wonderful thing to hear the voice of God within your person.

RAISE THE DEAD

Recently I read an account of Smith Wigglesworth proving the reality of the resurrection power of the Gospel of Jesus. He had an invitation to a gathering of friends of a man who had died. It was not the funeral. The body was in a side room behind two closed glass doors, in an open coffin. The guests gathered in a large main room. On arrival, Wigglesworth walked through the gathered group looking at everybody but not[saying a word. He reached the glass doors, opened them, and walked up to the coffin. He took hold of the clothing of the corpse, hauled the body out of the coffin, and stood it against a wall.

He stood back a few steps and said, "In the name of Jesus I command you to walk." The body slid slowly down the wall to the floor. Wigglesworth picked it up and stood it against the wall. Again, he said, "I command you to walk in the name of Jesus." The body slid slowly down the wall to the floor. He stood the body against the wall a third time and witnesses said this time he roared, "I command you to walk in the name of Jesus." The dead man's eyes fluttered open and he staggered forward. Witnesses said a short time later the resurrected man and Smith Wigglesworth walked arm in arm through the astonished group.

For those people present it was no doubt a life-changing event. You would not have been able to go on with 'life as usual' after witnessing such a spectacle. As ripples spread in a lake when a stone is thrown into it, the aftermath of the dead man alive again must have impacted many people. His family when he walked back into his house, the neighbours once the news reached them, his extended family, his workmates. If he turned up for work the next day that would have been something to see. When you think about it that one act of faith must have influenced a multitude of people.

We can think, "Isn't that wonderful, wasn't Wigglesworth a great man of faith". We should be alert to the fact you and I have a commandment — a commandment, not a suggestion — to do the very same thing. Jesus sent the twelve disciples out on an evangelistic outreach. (Mathew 10:5–8) "*These twelve Jesus sent out and commanded them saying, do not go into the way of the Gentiles and do not enter a city of the Samaritans. But go rather to the lost sheep of the house of Israel. And as you go preach, saying, the kingdom of heaven is at hand. Heal the sick, cleanse the lepers, raise the dead, cast out demons. Freely you have received, freely give.*"

Of that verse, some have said, "That was for the twelve disciples not us." If we go to the end of the book of Mathew we read; "*And Jesus came and spoke to them saying, All authority has been given to Me in heaven and on earth. Go therefore and make disciples of all the nations. Baptizing them in the name of the Father and of the Son and of the Holy Spirit. Teaching them to observe all things that I have commanded you; and lo, I am with you always, even to the end of the age.*" (Mathew 28;18–20)

We as Christians — and I am reminding myself here — need to be alert that we must not drift into "*Having the appearance of Godliness but denying it's power.*" (2 Tim 3:5) If we say we are disciples of Christ, these things are part of our job description. Our responsibility is to be available and ready to act. If you are thinking, 'Oh I could never do that.' It's good to remind ourselves that. "You have died, and your life is hidden with Christ in God." (Col 3:3) This commandment makes clear the division between 'religious' Christianity and true Christianity. True Christianity is a power life.

I heartily recommend the online Christian film 'Dead Raiser' if you have not yet come across it. (see it on video sites online) The offshoot of that documentary made by a group of young Christian leaders was the DRT — Dead Raising Teams Ministry. Tyler Johnson of www.oneglance.org and www.deadraisingteam.com — one of those young men, has been called to make the body of Christ aware of this part of our responsibility. His book, 'How to Raise the Dead' is available on Amazon. The Lord graciously appoints people to direct our attention to what is in every one of our Bibles.

The New Testament has a dead raising event that is far more spectacular than any of Wigglesworth's raisings. *"And Jesus cried out again with a loud voice and yielded up His spirit. Then behold, the veil of the Temple was torn in two from top to bottom: and the earth quaked, and the rocks split, and the graves opened; and many bodies of the saints who had fallen asleep were raised; and coming out of the graves after His resurrection, they went into the holy city and appeared to many."* (Mathew 27:50–53) I think this event is a display of God's eagerness to show the results of Jesus' sacrifice of Himself and His resurrection. It is as if God is saying, "Look here is proof of your salvation." It seems to be a preliminary to the final resurrection mentioned by Paul in 1Corinthians 15:52. *"...In a moment, in the twinkling of an eye, at the last trumpet. For the trumpet will sound, and the dead will be raised incorruptible, and we shall be changed..."*

Imagine you were walking past one of Jerusalem's cemeteries at the very moment this happened. Graves were open, and the occupants began to climb out and walk around. Then as you watched they headed towards the cemetery gate and made for various parts of the City. If you were brave enough and decided to follow some of them, you would have seen them knocking on doors around the City and looked on as astonished residents opened their doors to find a long-dead relative or friend standing there very much alive. Former acquaintances would have seen them passing and thought, "that looks like Moshe — no it can't be !" The word would have spread rapidly throughout Jerusalem because the verse tells us 'many' of the bodies of the saints were raised and appeared to 'many'.

I think long afterward those open graves would have been a witness in themselves. Many who had known those who had died and now lived, would see those open tombs and remember the death of that person whose grave was now empty.

A lot of questions come to mind when I read these verses. Parts of the passage happened when Jesus was on the cross and cried out — the rest of it happened after His resurrection. When Jesus yielded up His Spirit the earth quaked, rocks split, and the bodies of the Saints were raised. It wasn't until after His resurrection they came out of the graves and went into the City. It seems they were raised but lay in their graves until Christ's resurrection on the third day. Did the resurrected ones continue to live in Jerusalem or were they taken to Heaven? Who were these raised Saints? Were they well-known Old Testament characters? Was John the Baptist among them? God certainly chose a remarkable way to advertise the truth of Jesus's salvation.

David and Debbie Hogan have been Missionaries to the Indian people in the Jungles of North Mexico for more than twenty years. In that time more than 500 people have been raised from the dead. Most of those were Indians ministering to other Indians. David himself was raised to life after being beaten up and thrown into a river. These impoverished and uneducated people expect God to do these things. It is basic Gospel to them.

Jesus, as the firstborn from the dead, destroyed the devil who had the power of death through sin. Christ showed Himself to be the holy Son of God by His resurrection from the dead. He had never sinned. Therefore, death could not hold Him. The same power that raised Jesus from the dead is in our lives. Our call is to show that power as proof of the reality of the Gospel. (Rev1:5) (Heb 2:14) (Rom 1:4) (Ephes1:19,20) (Rom 15:19)

FIVE WAYS CHRISTIANS CAN HEAL THE SICK

I t is essential for us to always keep in mind Christianity is not just information. (1 Corinthians 4:20) *For the Kingdom of God is not a matter of words but of power.* Paul prayed, *That you might know what is the* exceeding greatness of His (God the Father) *power toward us who believe. (Ephesians chapter one)* The word 'know' in the New Testament means 'to have the experience of'. He goes on to say it is the same power that raised Jesus from the dead.

These five methods are as taught by Richard Roberts, son of Oral Roberts, and President of ORU University, Tulsa, Oklahoma. (2Timothy 2:2) *And the things you have heard me say in the presence of many witnesses entrust to reliable people who will also be qualified to teach others* . It is a Bible principle to teach others what we have been taught. That is what I am doing here.

Method one; *You shall lay hands on the sick and they shall recover.* (Mark 16:17,18) As Christians, we can put our hands on sick people, in Jesus' name, and expect God to heal them.

Method two: Speaking the Word. (Psalm 107:20) *He sent His Word and healed them, and delivered them from their destructions* . Richard Roberts suggests if we cannot for some reason get to the locality of a person we can say, "I send the Word of healing to ... Every sickness and disease come out in the name of Jesus."

Method three: Prayer cloths. Acts 19:11,12) Richard Roberts reminds us that Paul did this, and in fact cloths that had been on his body were laid on the sick and they recovered. Richard Roberts says," When I lay my hands on a cloth (any sort of cloth) my spiritual DNA goes into the cloth. It is a point of contact."

Method four: Anointing oil. The African Churches use this method a lot. Members of Churches carry small bottles of oil wherever they go and use it on themselves and for the sick. I heard the testimony of a young man who had anointing oil, that had been prayed over, in his pocket when the car he was travelling in had a serious accident. Others in the car were either killed or badly injured. The young man did not have a scratch on him. A lady dropped dead in her kitchen. Her husband came from work to the Hospital. He put the oil on her body, and she was raised to life after being declared dead for three or four hours. Any oil can be used and prayed over.

Method five: Pray for one another. (James 5:16) *Confess your faults one* to another, and pray one for another, that ye may be healed. *The effectual fervent prayer of a righteous man makes power available, dynamic in its working.* Richard Roberts calls this seed faith praying. When we have a need and pray for someone else, we sow a seed of faith that enables God to meet our needs. Everything we do for others is a seed that will come back to our benefit.

Richard Roberts does all these things in his close relationship with God. That is an important example for us. Ask, and let God direct you to heal the sick. I spent a month in Hospital recently for a serious condition. One thing I saw was that modern-day medicine does not always have all the answers. They can do a lot, but many sick people still need God's intervention. That intervention comes through you and me.

JOHN G LAKE AND HIS PANDEMIC

At his first Pastorate as a new Wesleyan Minister, John Lake decided he was more suited to business than the Ministry. He became a Manager of Agents for an Insurance Company. Not long after he opened a Real Estate office, helped start a Newspaper, bought a seat on the Chicago Board of Trade, and was Land Manager for a high-profile Railway Tycoon. In less than two years he was a wealthy man, respected for his ability to make money.

During this time he was having many wonderful experiences with God, was praying for the sick with marvellous results, and eventually preaching almost every night of the week. At this time, it came to the point where in his words, "my heart was divided." The desire to win souls to Christ began to interfere with his success at business. Business appointments where a short interview would have produced a significant amount of money became conversations concerning the soul of the visitor. He took a three-month vacation from business, began full-time evangelistic ministry, which included praying for the sick wherever there was a need. He did not return to the Business World.

At the close of the three months, "I disposed of my Estate and distributed my funds in a manner I believed to be in the best interests of the Kingdom of God. I resolved to make myself and my family completely dependent upon God for support and abandoned myself to the preaching of Jesus." In April of 1908, the call of God came to go to Africa. With his wife, seven children, and four others, they set out by faith. After purchasing the tickets for the passage, they were left with $1.50 for expenses. God provided in many wonderful ways, not the least being the provision of a house in Johannesburg when they landed.

Books have been written of Hundreds of Churches started and thousands of souls saved, and sick healed, in the five short years, the Lake family was in Africa. In 1910 a disease known as African fever, believed to be smallpox, killed one-quarter of the black and white populations of two districts. Bubonic plague was also in the areas where John Lake ministered. He stayed in the field to pray and help in every manner he could. He tells of helping with the sick until his clothes were covered in the pus and discharge of the disease. His practise then was to wade into a river fully clothed, wash all the discharge from his clothes, then return to the task.

Stories of his apparent immunity to disease began to spread and many medical and scientific researchers came from international destinations to observe and interview Lake. On one occasion he wiped the toxic foam from the mouth of a victim and asked a group of scientists to view his hand under a microscope. The disease microbes were seen to be dying as soon as they came into contact with John Lakes' skin.

In one of his later sermons, Lake explains that the Law of sin and death, from whence disease comes, is no match for the law of the Spirit of life in Christ Jesus in every Christian. Roberts Liardon has collected all of John Lakes sermons in one book which is available online.. Other books about the life of John G Lake are available from various retailers. The older books can be sourced from Openlibrary.org. A study of Lakes' life and sermons will give you a whole new perspective on the life and victory Jesus has given us.

JESUS ATE AND DRANK WITH SINNERS

Jesus ate and drank with sinners, so the Gospels tell us. Probably the equivalent of our meeting at Starbucks for coffee.

A while ago I read some advice to Christians for handling contact with the World's uncleanliness. Get away from it lest you be contaminated, was the advice in brief. Is that the mind set we should have?

I don't think so. Obviously, we should not go looking for contact with the many instances of impurity in the World. We can change channels on the TV, choose not to read ugh! stuff, and stay away from places exceedingly sinful, if we are not going there to preach the Gospel. But what about the many situations where I can't get away?

I had a situation not too long ago where I was working with a self-employed person, just the two of us together every day. He knew I was a Christian and I spoke openly about the Lord. This guy was not in the least bothered about me being a Christian. He continued with his normal conversation of dirty jokes and generally off !! conversation. I couldn't get away, I had to work with him for three months. At the end of that three months I discovered why God had me with this guy. He admitted he had received Jesus when he was younger. I think God had me there as a prod to him, to get himself right with God.

I worked for years in the Construction Industry. I have been in that situation many times before. It took me a while to learn, but now my first thought is always, "Here is a sinner Jesus died for. He is still alive so God is not holding his sins against him, but has already forgiven him in Christ, if he will accept it'"

Secondly I remind myself of Mark 7:18 where Jesus says *"Are you thus without understanding also? Do you not perceive that whatever enters a man from the outside cannot defile him, because it does not enter his heart"*.....He goes on to say the contents of a person's heart and what comes out of it, is what defiles them. Since God has provided me with a pure heart through Jesus' salvation, I don't have to be concerned about being contaminated. During that three month stint God also gave me grace to handle the situation. You do need, though, to be open about being a Christian and a follower of Jesus.

It is important and life is so much easier, if we have received the pure heart that Jesus obtained for us by His suffering, death, burial, and resurrection. Unfortunately, not all believers know that is available. Acts 15 records an incident where Peter preaches the Gospel to a group of Gentiles. The Holy Spirit is given to them, and their hearts are purified by faith. The first Christians expected that to happen when the Holy Spirit turned up. Jesus also said, *"blessed are the pure in heart"*.

I think many Christians unconsciously think Jesus meant "blessed are those who make their heart clean." Some think we have to strive to get rid of sin. That is error. If we could do those things we could pat ourselves on the back and say, "well I'm better than many others." Human effort is not part of the Gospel. The only work that will ever count is the work Christ did in the Garden and on the Cross. His is a finished work to be received by faith.

Speaking of the heart in Luke 6, Jesus said a good tree cannot bear bad fruit. We can go out into the world knowing what God has made clean cannot be made unclean. We can then focus on praying for, and winning the lost to the Gospel.

THE PROOF YOU ARE A CHRISTIAN.

" *We know, said John the apostle, that we have passed over out of death and into life because we love our fellow Christians".* (1John 3:14) The question then arises, what is love? Jesus, in the book of Luke, gives us some ideas about that.

"Give to everyone who asks of you. And from him who takes away your goods do not ask them back. And just as you want men to do to you, you also do to them likewise. But if you love those who love you, what credit is that to you? For even sinner's love those who love them. And if you lend to those from whom you hope to receive back, what credit is that to you? For even sinners lend to sinners to receive as much back. But love your enemies, do good, and lend, hoping for nothing in return; and your reward will be great, and you will be sons of the Highest. For He is kind to the unthankful and evil. Therefore, be merciful, just as your Father also is merciful". (Luke 6:30–36)

God has given us one whole chapter in the New Testament to make it clear to us what love is. That chapter is 1Corinthians 13. If we do not take serious note of this information we will not be living as God expects us to. A warning: your flesh (humanity) will not like what God teaches us in this chapter. A good time to remind ourselves many of us were unlovely before we were saved. The New Testament says God is love (1John 4:8) As Christians, we have Gods love in us through the Holy Spirit.

"Now hope does not disappoint because the love of God has been poured out into our hearts by the Holy Spirit who was given unto us". (Rom 5:5) Love is a Spiritual condition. Along with me, it probably did not take you long to realize that your humanity does a bad job of

loving God's way. Love is a choice to live from our spirits. *"The fruit of the Spirit is love".* (Gal 5:22)

I encourage you to keep the importance of living in God's love first among your spiritual priorities. Here are two ways I have discovered that help me to be love minded. Many years ago, Edwin Markham, a poet, wrote these words. "He drew a circle that shut me out — heretic, rebel, a thing to flout. But love and I had the wit to win; We drew a circle and included him in".

Jesus appeared to a man named Star Daily, a career criminal, in prison, in solitary confinement, in the early 1900's. He had been a gangster who worked for Al Capone. He became a writer and a man of love. In the years before he was released, he worked tirelessly to bring the love of God to fellow prisoners. He wrote these words about God's omnipresence, in his book 'Love Can Open Prison Doors' (reprint available at online retailers)

"We swim in an infinite ocean of love. To become increasingly conscious of our oneness with love, is the mark of exercising intelligent self-interest. To this end, we do not labour and strain in our search for love. It is above, beneath, and about us. It is seeking us".

I find meditating on the above quote changes my perceptions about God, and my attitude to people.

The apostle Paul said," *Make love your great quest".* (I Cor 14:1)

BEAMING FOR JESUS

*L*et *your light so shine before men, that they may see your good works, and glorify your Father which is in heaven.* (Math 5:16) Notice the presupposition here by Jesus; your light. With this directive from Jesus in mind, this story sets out to answer the questions; what does being a light in the world look like? How do I know I am fulfilling this part of Scripture? What more could we be doing to be a light in the world?

"But the secret of Christianity is not in doing; the secret is in being." John G Lake's counsel for a successful Christian life. It is also the starting line to being a light for God in the world. The Living Bible tells us when Jesus came, *the true light arrived to shine on everyone coming into the World. (John 1:9)* He declared it of Himself, *"I am the light of the world."* Nine times in the first chapter, the Gospel of John calls Jesus the light. Light came into this world as a person, Christ. was the light of men. *And the light shines in the darkness, and the darkness did not comprehend it. In Him (Jesus) was life and the life was the light of men.* (John 1:4,5)

The true light, as John calls it, came into the world in the person and character of Jesus. Light was a person. It is the same for us today, light is a person, you and me. True light is not some spiritual essence existing as a force or substance floating out there somewhere. True light is embodied in people. Light is the nature and character of Christ in us, His people.

Jesus handed the baton to us as His people when He said, You are the light of the World. (Math 5:14) Wow! big responsibility! Well ?...Yes and no. Ephesians 5:8 eases the burden, For you were once darkness, but now you are light in the Lord... No further action is required. We have returned to John G Lakes' comment, being, not doing is the secret of Christianity. Paul confirmed it by saying, *...in the midst of a crooked and perverse generation, among whom you shine as lights in the World.* To paraphrase; your acceptance of Jesus as saviour means you shine when you are among the unsaved. (Phil 2:15)

If you want to be comfortable in your life among unsaved people you should start by agreeing with God that you are a light for Him. It's Martin Luther's formula again. God said it, I believe it, that settles it. That is faith. Earlier in my Christian walk, I let discouragement get to me because it seemed nobody was noticing my light. The realization that many missed seeing Jesus, the Son of God, in a sinless body, for who He was, helped me. As I accepted by faith, I was a light, I relaxed and eventually began to see it was happening.

Occasionally, people who did not know I was a Christian have apologized for their attitude or something they said in my presence. Of course, people see your light clearly when you are talking about Jesus, or it becomes known you are a committed Christian. I have listened to workmates give the usual long diatribe about Christians being hypocrites, and all that is wrong with the Church, then finish with "of course, it's different with you, you're a real Christian." All I had done was attempt to project love and not compromise on righteousness.

The reverse is true for the world. The darkness of the world is in the nature and character of the people. Once you were darkness, Paul (Phil 2:15). John chapter one tells us, *And the light shines in the darkness, and the darkness did not comprehend it.* A little further on we read, *He came to His own and His own received Him not.* Jesus the light came to the darkness, the people of the world, and the darkness comprehended Him not. (2 Cor 6:14) *Do not be unequally yoked with unbelievers...what communion has light with darkness.* Again, equating light and darkness with people.

We are light. Jesus's statement is emphatic, You are the light of the world. We can get more from Mathew 5:16. *Let your light so shine before men that they may see your good works and glorify your Father in heaven.* He wants our light to be revealed in a specific manner.

I believe part of that is our manifestation of the character of Jesus. In a world immersed in me, myself, and I, the character or nature of God is a bright beacon. You may be thinking, "am I able to do that?" What does the Word say? *...Love has been perfected among us in this.....because as He is, so are we in this world."* (1John 4:17) We have come back to faith again. Paul couples light with character in Phil 2:15, *Do all things without complaining and disputing, that you may become blameless and harmless, children of God without fault in the midst of a crooked and perverse generation, among whom you shine as lights in a dark world.* This, he says, is how to let your light be seen.

John also connects light with the divine character, the spiritual life of Christ within us. He who says he is in the light and hates his brother, is in darkness until now. He who loves his brother abides in the light, and there is no cause for stumbling in him. (1John 1:9,10) According to John if we are living that way we are walking in the light. (1John 1:7, 2:10)

Peter makes it of first importance in his second letter. Grace and peace be multiplied to you in the knowledge of God and of Jesus our Lord, as His divine power has given to us all things that pertain to life and godliness, through the knowledge of Him who called us by glory and virtue, by which have been given to us exceedingly great and precious promises, that through these you may be partakers of the divine nature, having escaped the corruption that is in the world through lust. Again, a matter of faith. All things needed for life and living for God, have been given to us.

IT'S NOT HARD TO BE HOLY

If I asked you, "Are you a holy person"? What would your answer be? I think most of us would hesitate and not be sure how to respond. Many Christians are not sure of themselves when it comes to holiness. That is curious if you think about it, because we are Sons and Daughters of the Holy God. The Spirit we have within us is the Holy Spirit. Here are 8 facts from the Bible too give you a better understanding about holiness.

God commands us to be holy: ...'because it is written', "Be holy for I am holy". (1Pet 1:16)

Paul had no doubt that you and I are holy: 'God chose us in Jesus Christ before the foundation of the world, that we should be holy and without blame before Him in love'. (Eph 1:4) If you had asked him, "Paul are you holy"? "Yes, I am", he would have replied, "Come and meet some of my fellow Christians, they are holy too".

A life of holiness has been prepared for us: God showed Isaiah a Holy Highway that had been prepared especially for Christians. 'And a highway shall be there and a way, and it shall be called the holy way....it shall be for the redeemed....the redeemed shall walk upon it'. (Is 35:8,9)

It is not hard to be holy: God has something surprising to say about walking on the holy highway: 'The highway shall be for the redeemed; the wayfaring men, yes, the simple ones and fools, shall not make a mistake in it and lose their way'. (Is 35:8) A simple minded person and even fools can succeed at holy living. Is God trying to tell us something here? I think so. It's not hard to be holy.

Holiness is a gift to be received: '...much more those who receive abundance of grace and of the gift of righteousness shall reign in life through the One, Jesus Christ'. (Rom 5:17) The word translated as holiness in the New Testament, can also be translated as purity and righteousness.

Holiness is our reward for receiving Jesus as our saviour: *'But now since you have been set free from sin and become slaves of God, you have your present reward in holiness and its end is eternal life.'* (Rom 6:22)

Holiness is a pure heart, freed from sin: *'And God, who knows the heart, bore witness to them, giving them the Holy Spirit as also He did to us; and He made no difference between us and them, but purified their hearts by faith'.* (Acts 15:8,9) *'To the pure in heart all things are pure'.* (Tit 1:15)

A pure heart is received by faith: *'And God....purified their hearts by faith'.* (Acts 15:8,9

The New Testament has a lot more to say about holiness. I encourage you to spend time with God, asking Him to teach you all there is to know about holiness. We can be as certain as Paul was, that we are holy.

SECRETS OF A SUCCESSFUL MARRIAGE

IT MIGHT SURPRISE YOU to know the Bible book of Malachi is a great source book for Marriage Counselling. You could say the theme of the book is God's troubled marriage to Israel. Of course, the trouble is not on God's side. Here is Malachi 1:1 *The burden of the word of the Lord to Israel by Malachi. I have loved you says the Lord. Yet you say, 'in what way have you loved us?'* You know a marriage is in trouble when one of the partners has forgotten the love that once was alive between them. God is obliged to remind them of the history of His relationship with Israel and all He had done to create a love union with them.

We often think that God's word by Malachi in 3:8–10 *Will a man rob God? Yet you have robbed me! But you say, in what way have we robbed you? In tithes and offerings. You are cursed with a curse. For you have robbed me. Even this whole nation, Bring all the tithes into the storehouse. That there may be food in my house—* Is a rebuke to the people for not bringing their tithes to God. If we go back in the book, we find that was not the case. The people and the priests were giving tithes and offerings at the correct times under the law. The problem is revealed in Malachi 1:7–8 *You offer defiled food on my altar, but say, in what way have we defiled you? By saying the table of the Lord is contemptible. And when you offer the blind as a sacrifice, is it not evil? And when you offer the lame and sick, is it not evil? Offer it then to your governor. Would he be pleased with you? Would he accept you favourably? Says the Lord of Hosts.*

God was expecting them to obey the law by enthusiastically and cheerfully bringing Him tithes and offerings of the best of everything. Instead, they were offering defiled offerings and giving the Lord animals that were of no value to them because of sickness, blindness, and being lame. What has that to do with marriage? The relationship on Israel's side had broken down to a lifeless thing. They were merely going through the form of meeting the law — but the way they did that was an insult to God and an affront to His love for them. They had an attitude problem. God had expected them to keep their side of the love relationship. Instead, they had allowed an attitude of deadness and rejection to creep in. They were robbing Him with defiled tithes and offerings, and robbing Him of the love response He deserved.

If we look through the book we find words that are very applicable to the maintenance of a loving relationship — Marriage. Honour was missing. (1:6) Reverence was missing. (1:6) The people had begun to speak contemptuously about the relationship. (1:7) They were saying, "O what a weariness this relationship is." (1:13) The fear of God was missing. (1:14) They were not taking to heart the importance of the relationship. (2:2) They had ceased to regard the word of God about the relationship. (2:6) Godly knowledge and the ways of God had been rejected. (2:7,9) They had ceased to regard the relationship as a holy institution. (2:11) Their attitude was blocking answers to their prayers. (2:13) The people had begun to despise the covenant involved in the relationship. (2:14)

God also reminds the Israelites of the many blessings that come from Him when they put effort and delight into keeping the relationship. The windows of heaven will be opened, and a blessing poured out that cannot be contained. (3:10) He will rebuke the devourer for their sakes. (3:11) They will be prosperous, and people will notice they are blessed. (3:12) The Lord will look on them as His jewels. (3:17) Healing shall come to them. (4:2) Authority to trample the wicked will be given to them. (4:3)

Having absorbed the wisdom from Malachi we should now turn to the New Testament and 1Corinthians 13. We Christian's have a power within us that is missing in the World. Namely the love of God. (Rom 5:5) *Now hope does not disappoint, because the love of God has been shed abroad in our hearts by the Holy Spirit who has been given unto us.* 1Corinthians 13 is a description of that love in action. I have always thought one statement in the chapter is key to living in love. (Amplified Bible) *Love does not take into account a wrong done to it.* In my thinking a very necessary ingredient for a successful marriage. An Apostolic mentor of mine often said people come in two types. Those who are thick-skinned and those who are thin-skinned. Thick-skinned being a metaphor for people who don't easily take offense, thin-skinned for folks sensitive to rejections and wrongs done to them,

I did not want to admit it for a long time but finally had to face that I am of the thin-skinned variety. I found that subconsciously I accumulated a list in my mind of people or organizations who were at fault in some way in regard to my values or who had done the wrong thing by me. Thin-skinned out of control is no help in having a happy marriage. It was always a concern hovering in the back of my mind because I knew what 1Corinthians 13 said and I knew the practise of love was a major indicator of our new life. Also, there is that all-encompassing verse from 2Corinthians 5:19 That is that God was in Christ reconciling the world unto Himself, not imputing their trespasses to them, and has committed to us the word of reconciliation. The Lord has forgiven everybody in Christ. They only need to receive it. Only a few days ago I heard and saw an amazing testimony of a man who had been a violent criminal, drug smuggler, and fifteen-year drug addict. By God's mercy and patience, he came to Christ, and now after only nine years is a man of love and a Prophetic leader.

I have heard it said by preachers that one word from God can change your life. I have proved that to be true. Only a short while ago God bought two words to my attention — accuse and excuse. He told me they were opposites, and that excuse has the same meaning as forgive. Being a long-time Christian, the word forgive becomes commonplace and it takes quite a bit of mental activity to apply it to people or situations. He showed me if I said "I excuse them" it had the same meaning as forgiving. I started saying or thinking "I excuse them" to every situation that had previously disturbed me. It took two or three days to work through the subconscious list of grievances I was not fully aware I was holding. That practise brought a tremendous change and rest to my life. To make it work you need to stay alert to your responses and have a heart determination to persist. Eventually, it becomes a habit and happens automatically. You have become transformed by the renewing of your mind. I strongly recommend it for married couples who have knowingly or unknowingly accumulated some offense issues in their relationship.

That leads to another basic truth of our Christian life. Colossians 3:3 puts it this way. For you are dead and your (true real-Amplified Bible) life is hid with Christ in God. The truth is — the part of us that takes offense and is touchy and easily hurt died with Christ at Calvary. If we take that on board as a fundamental reality of our Christian lives, we will be more alert to letting our Christ selves come to the front in all our living. It is a truth that I think many Christians miss. We are not to carry on living as we did before, as singular human selves. You are dead is a strong statement. It needs meditation and commitment to accept it as a spiritual reality. God made it work for me by giving the 'I excuse' formula. He may do it differently for you. We are on a battleground in this World, and we need to succeed in getting past our humanity into the Christ life within us.

I should say also when I began applying the 'I excuse' formula it opened the way for the love and kindness and patience of God to come out in my life. I am much more tolerant of obstacles and life's petty frustrations. I notice I am more spontaneously friendly and communicative with people. I guess I should not be too surprised —

to have our lives hid with Christ in God is an awesome and powerful reality.

FEW HAVE DISCOVERED THIS BIBLE VERSE

Once we become Christians the quality of our Christian life depends on two things. Our knowledge of the Bible, and our faith in God's Word therein. Some may respond 'what about our relationship with God?' Jesus mysteriously identified Himself with the Bible in the Book of Hebrews 10:7 *Then I (Jesus) said, 'Behold, I have come — In the volume of the book it is written of Me — To do Your will, O God.'* He was meaning the actual physical Bible here when He said 'the volume of the Book'. Jesus always included the Word of God in His relationship with His Father.

It's the same with us. The quality of our relationship with The Father, The Son' and the Holy Spirit, and the successful Christian life, depends on our knowledge of the Bible, and our faith in it as God's Word. When you think about it what do you have if every aspect of your life is not based on an understanding of the Bible? Our own imaginations. A very dodgy foundation!

The passage of my title is Hebrews 10:1–4: (NKJB) *For the law, having a shadow of the good things to come, and not the very image of the things, can never with these same sacrifices, which they offer continually year by year, make those who approach perfect. For then would they not have ceased to be offered? For the worshipers, once purified, would have had no more consciousness of sins. But in those sacrifices there is a reminder of sins every year. For it is not possible that the blood of bulls and goats could take away sins.*

It is a radical passage. Not radical from God's point of view, but radical to the general beliefs of a lot of the body of Christ. The objection can often come up with passages like this that it was a mistake of the translators. So I will put that to rest first. 14 Translations have the exact same wording as I am using here, and the rest have the same meaning but with alternate English words.

Put simply, this passage is saying the sacrifices under the Law had to be enacted over and over again, and with all that activity sin was never permanently dealt with. The theme of the passage and of a lot of the Book of Hebrews, is that Jesus took away sin once and for all by His one- time sacrifice of Himself. Did you notice what the result of Jesus' sacrifice is for those who worship Him? They are purified and have no more consciousness of sins. Those results are described as the good things to come. Hey! that's radical! God's response would be, "Not for me, it's been in the Bible from the beginning. I expect you to believe it. That's why I put it there, to inform you of what you have in Jesus."

Somewhere along the line a few people, not being able to handle the immensity of What Christ did for us, began to inject their own ideas into their teaching. It spread rapidly: Christians are still sinners, Christians must confess sins every-day, Christians are not perfect just forgiven etc etc. They even changed some Bible translations to suit their erroneous teaching. What we need to grasp is this was a work of God through His divine Son Jesus. God never does shoddy work. We need to come up to God's revelation of what has been done to us and for us. Too many have pulled it down and substituted human ideas instead.

I read of one guy who discovered these verses and was shocked. It was not what his denomination taught. Instead of going to God about it he started asking other Christians and leaders what they thought. One thing that came out of it was his discovery some weird ideas are out there about Christians and sin. Whether he finally went to God I don't know. The answer to his shock is in James 1:5 If any of you lacks wisdom, let him ask of God, who gives to all liberally and without reproach, and it will be given to him.

GIVING THANKS MIGHT BE YOUR ANSWER

A few days ago I was reminded again of the benefits of responding to an instruction God has given us in the New Testament. I had been bugged for a month with a physical ailment. I had prayed about it, believed concerning it, and done all the Bible tells us Christians to do when we encounter problems of any kind. I remembered I had missed one clear instruction God gives us in a number of places in the New Testament.

1 Thessalonians 5:16–18 Rejoice always, pray continually, give thanks in all circumstances; for this is God's will for you in Christ Jesus.

I gave thanks for it and bingo! it was gone. It is an instruction, which means obedience is involved. When we became Christian's we committed ourselves to living God's way. God's way is revealed to us in the Bible. The details are there for us to respond to.

Meditating on this verse I came up with these facts. Firstly, it says in all circumstances. That means good or bad. Pleasant experiences and unpleasant experiences. 'All' means all. It is to be a response to God peculiar to Christians. A part of the life we now live, different from the rest of the World. It something that marks the life of those who are 'in Christ Jesus'.

Like the Nike slogan, we are told just to do it. Doesn't matter if you don't understand why God would tell us to do such a thing. Doesn't matter whether you feel like it or not. Doesn't matter if you do it begrudgingly through clenched teeth and pursed lips. (I have found the more severe the circumstance the more resistance I feel to obeying this instruction.) Doesn't say spend a half day thanking God, or an hour, or five minutes. It just says do it!

In my opinion we need only say it once, "Thank you God for this circumstance, problem — whatever." Then we have obeyed and done the will of God. I find if I reluctantly squeeze one "thank you" out of my mouth it creates a freedom, and I will often find myself thinking of all the needs in my life and thanking God for all of them — as well as the many good things.

It goes against the grain of our human thinking and feeling. But Hey! that's what the Christian life is all about. You will find other references to being thankful here : Colossians 2:6–7, James 1:17, Hebrews 12:28, Philippians 4:4–7, Colossians 3:15–17, Ephesians 5:18–20, Hebrews 13:15, 2Corinthians 9:15.

When you have done it, rest assured God has taken notice you have responded to his will. If the result you hoped for is not immediate hang in there and you will eventually see the benefit. Just do it!

THE END